Faith Healing Explained

How Then Shall We Pray, Volume 3

Brother Eric

Published by Brother Eric, 2023.

Faith Healing Explained

Miracles vs unanswered prayer

Brother Eric

BROTHER ERIC

Bible Quotations

All Scripture quotations are from the *New King James Version NKJV* unless otherwise indicated: Copyright © 1982 by Thomas Nelson, Inc. Used by permission. All rights reserved.

Scripture quotations indicated *NIV* are taken from: THE HOLY BIBLE, NEW INTERNATIONAL VERSION®, NIV® Copyright © 1973, 1978, 1984, 2011 by Biblica, Inc.™ Used by permission. All rights reserved worldwide.

Scripture quotations indicated *WEB* are taken from the *WORLD ENGLISH BIBLE*.

The *World English Bible* is in the Public Domain. "*World English Bible*" is a Trademark of eBible.org.

Author Eric and wife Petré outside a church in Masan, South Korea, where they served in the English service from 2015 to 2017.

Also by the author:

Pyongyang Again Jerusalem of the East – *Prayer, prophets and deals*

The Songbird-bride from Mumbai – *A faith-based musical*

Future Royal Israel series – *The Gathering After the Church Age*

PARTISIE – (*Partition – The ZA rebirth*)

My story – a passion for truth

HOW did I, as a journalist by trade, become an 'investigative author' in a world where everyone has an opinion and theologians fiercely argue doctrines? What drives a passion for truth, as per John 4:24?

It started in 1990. While running the Comrades ultra-marathon, I saw a small airplane dragging a message that read: 'Come unto Me said Jesus,' but being a regular Christian in a Calvinist-Protestant culture, it took a friend months to convince me, that like a Nicodemus, one must become born again.

A calling to write and a quest for truth caused an intensive, Berean-like, daily study of Scriptures with an entire-Word approach, resulted in *'the Future Royal Israel series,' 'How then shall we Pray?'* and other books.

Having been married since 1982, we have four sons. My maternal heritage traces back to the first free Dutch pioneers in South Africa in 1657 and on my paternal side to the famous Protestant John Bodley, with possible links through to 17th century Jewry in Germany, from where my grandfather came.

This probably explains a great, probably genetic, love for Israel. Thus, should you ask: "Are you Protestant, Evangelic or Messianic?" The answer is: "Neither, I'm all of above!"

Shalom, beloved in Yeshua.

Brother Eric, revised 8/2023.

With gratitude to those fellow believers who have prayed with and for us over many years. The plowmen opening the fallow ground for the reapers (1 Corinthians 9:10; Amos 9:13).

The Divine Reason for faith-healing

Is unanswered prayer for healing not perhaps the greatest disappointment of religion?

Most believers, even the very sincere and pious, lack in confidence because of teachings and doctrines that make excuses for the lack of faith and the absence of miracles! The other side of the coin are those who are taught to "decree" and "confess" miracles and then, when silence is the answer, are at a loss and even lose faith.

To pray is a privilege and we need to 'press in,' for the Kingdom is taken with power, but beware of being dogmatic. Can the clay tell the potter? (Isa. 64:8; Rom. 9:21). No, we do not prescribe, but the righteous can, as in the parable of the persistent widow; ask with confidence (Luke 18:1-8).

Believers need to gain greater confidence in the willingness of our God, for thousands of healing miracles do occur, but the divine reason must be understood.

Believers must press in with faith regardless when tested, knowing that victory is both in healing and in bearing the cross.

Countering the Apostacy

There is a vulnerability among Christians to an eclectic spirituality, each galloping into the battle as they please, to echo the words of Jeremiah: *"I listened and heard, but they didn't speak right... everyone turns to his course, as a horse that rushes headlong in the battle"* (Jeremiah 8:6).

The original 'How then shall we Pray? 80 core essence issues' (2016) was birthed to counter ignorance, apostasy, Spirituality and New Age methodology, the mixing of the Gospel with the occult.

The call is to re-examine both old assumptions and new habits of the faith, not to judge unfairly (Luke 6:35-37), but to *"strengthen the lame"* (Hebrews 12:12), and to speak out against those who *"muddy the water"* (Ezekiel 34:17-19, NIV).

Many millions are simply following religious traditions and so miss *"God's purpose for themselves"* (Luke 7:30). Worse, however, is the antinomian or neo-Nicolaitan apostacy, the pernicious teaching of Progressives promoting worldly, self-centered doctrines in conflict with Scripture (Mat. 7:22-23; Rev. 2:6, 15).

The call is for God-fearing reverence, to respect God's opinion on matters, as revealed in the Bible, with faith and the power of Spirit, to cast out the idols of doctrines (1 John 5:21). The challenge is not to lose our *"first Love"* (Revelation 2:2-4), but to grow in *"truth and Spirit"* (John 4:24), and a fresh expectancy for the Kingdom of Messiah (Mark 7:34).

The challenge is to explain our instinctive love for *"the Land of Immanuel"* (Isaiah 8:8), for there is a day coming when, *"the earth shall be filled with the knowledge of the glory of the LORD [YeHoVaH], as the waters cover the sea"* (Habakkuk 2:14).

Part 1 Praying for healing

INDEX

1. Is faith-healing always Plan A?

"DON'T write a book with ten reasons on why God doesn't heal! Healing is God's Plan A, there is no Plan B!" This bold but incorrect statement came from Pastor Dan Mohler, a man with amazing testimonies regarding prayer for healing. He replied to the question of why only some people get healed by prayer. [i]

"We've made this far more difficult than what it is; (thinking) that it's about praying better prayers, more spiritual prayers, emphasizing the name of Jesus...

"Jesus is not synonymous with abracadabra. He's the name above every name. Faith is not a method; prayer is not why men get healed, believing in the finished work of Christ is why men are healed! It has nothing to do with what you pray, but all about what you believe!

"We have turned this into us (instead of God) and got so self-conscious that people do not want to pray for the sick. We try to fill something that's already complete," is how Pastor Dan explained it in one of the many of his sermons posted on *YouTube*.

Dan Mohler

Dan Mohler reminds one of the old Awakening preachers: he teaches from the heart for hours, has no 'ministry office,' and takes no travel reimbursement or appearance fees to teach across America.

Mohler's brazen critics clearly do not know his testimony, of what tests in life he has passed, about *"the lion and bear"* that has shaped him and his message (1 Sam. 17:34-37).

"We have thirty reasons why people are not healed. I'm sure Jesus did not have that book in his back pocket, because it was not His experience. If you accept any of those reasons, you have just placed a ceiling on top of what God can do. You've just stopped yourself from believing and growing past that reason."

FAITH HEALING EXPLAINED

This is a commonly held, but short-sighted view among Evangelicals, for it does not answer the disappointment of millions when their prayers go unanswered.

Neither does it provide believing Christians with an apology, an explanation to counter the cynical views of the world who dismiss faith or prayer healing as 'pseudoscience,' the placebo effect, illusions, hypnosis or pure fraudulent showmanship – especially when an audience and cameras are present.

From the Protestant viewpoint, faith-healing through prayer has not been better motivated than the famous Andrew Murray who championed the Awakening in the Cape Colony (Southern Africa) in 1860. He was healed through prayer after suffering a break of two years in his ministry because of illness.

Murray famously said, "God, in the mystery of prayer, has entrusted us with a force that can move the heavenly world, and can bring its power down to earth."

In his book 'Divine Healing' (1890) Murray wrote: "I have clearly seen that the Church possesses in Jesus, our Divine Healer, an inestimable treasure, which she does not yet know how to appreciate.

"I have been convinced anew of that which the Word of God teaches us in this matter, and of what the Lord expects of us; and I am sure that if Christians learned to realize practically the presence of the Lord that heals, their spiritual life would thereby be developed and sanctified. I can therefore no longer keep silence.

"The Lord spoke to the disciples of divers sufferings which they should have to bear, but when He speaks of sickness, it is always as of an evil caused by sin and Satan, and from which we should be delivered. He declared that every disciple of His would have to bear his cross (Matt. 16:24), but He never taught one sick person to resign himself to be sick.

Jesus came to deliver men from sin and sickness that He might make known the love of the Father.

"Everywhere Jesus healed the sick, everywhere He dealt with healing as one of the graces belonging to the kingdom of heaven. Sin in the soul and sickness in the body both bear witness to the power of Satan, and *"the Son of God was manifested that he might destroy the works of the devil"* (I John 3:8).

Andrew Murray (1828-1917)

Believing in the continuation of the 'apostolic gifts' of the Holy Spirit against strong Calvinistic opposition in South Africa, Andrew Murray is described as a 'significant forerunner' of the Pentecostal movement, which is said to have started in America with Azusa Street, Los Angeles in 1906. He authored 240 works of which the majority are still very relevant. Author Olea Nel, the foremost expert on Murray, recounted the miracle start of the Cape Awakening in 1860 in both his Dutch Reformed congregation and the Anglican church in Wellington, 70 kilometers (44 miles) from Cape Town.

It is for this reason that divine healing manifests: It always points towards grace in Yeshua, the Holy Spirit being present in the love of our Heavenly Father.

Many are, unfortunately, like the poor madman of Gadara (Mark 5:1-20), so tormented by pain that they become self-destructive and do not want to be healed.

In unfaith, or driven by demon and pain, they flee from the Redeemer, incapable of understanding the depth of His love and compassion, underestimating God's great ability to heal and restore completely.

Many healings are not talked about. Like a neighbor who drank a bottle of of whiskey a day, and then in desperation one day prayed and immediately got released from the alcohol addiction, permanently and with no side-effects. There are smokers and drug addicts with similar testimonies.

But then there are cases – many in fact, where handmaidens and servants of the Almighty get tested by disease and they do not get prayers answered, much like Paul's *"thorn in the flesh,"* just more life-threatening. People whose faith and testimony are on par, or even better than that of the most flamboyant healing pastor. Those cases dare NOT be ignored, as most healing preachers do.

2. Why are the hospitals not empty?

"IF God answers prayer for healing, why are the hospitals not empty?" This is the cynical question the unbelieving world throws at the believer. Is unanswered prayer for healing not perhaps the greatest disappointment of religion?

Are the poor (observed) results of prayer not perhaps why so many unrepentant millions have no faith, thinking that there is no God out there? Is the Almighty deaf, or are we just dealing with Jewish fables, as atheists think?

No, of course not, but how do we explain it? Not to the scoffers, but to the brethren who are suffering with disability and pain.

"Come down from the cross!" the ignorant mocked Jesus (Mat. 27:30), clueless regarding the greater Kingdom-perspective for His suffering. Equally so is any attempt to prescribe how and where healing should take place.

The answer is that "Plan A" is God-sized and Kingdom-sized and not man-sized. The open prison door did not make Peter, Paul and Silas better saints than John the Baptist, or James, who got beheaded (Mat. 14:3-10; Acts 12:1-17, 16:23-26).

How do they explain the case of the powerful prophet Elisha? We don't see him plead for a longer life, yet a mysterious and unique event occurred when the body of a dead man came to life when it was hurriedly dumped in the prophet's tomb (2 Kings 13:14-25).

Was there healing power in the bones of Elisha? Imagine what fake healers would do if they could get hold of such "miracle bones"! No, it was a reminder from the grave for king Joash/ Jehoash of Israel of the prophet's words, spurring their faith to three promised victories against the Syrians.

Faith healing through prayer is thus not a topic for ignorant, simple answers. There is a martyr's roll that we do not seek, but sometimes have to bear, and in so doing, identify with Christ in His suffering and His glory, when our prayers are answered, but not the way we have expected.

For the 'sons of God' there is only victory: either with joyous Kingdom-advancing healing, which is fantastic, but temporary; or with the permanent honor of sharing in the suffering of Christ (John 1:12-13; Rom. 8:14-19; 1 John 3:1-2).

Either way: Be it in healing or in the somber reality of suffering; death has been defeated at the Cross: *"Now he is not the God of the dead, but of the living, for all are alive to him"* (Luke 20:38).

Sickness is a foothold the Adversary has gained by deceiving the first Adam, which is why Yeshua, as the Last Adam came to take the stripes (Isa. 53:4-5; Mat. 8:16-17; 1 Cor. 15:45-49). Through Yeshua is the brokenness, pain and sorrow – everything the enemy throws at us – turned to our advantage, for none of these afflictions can snatch the believer from our King Messiah (John 16:33; Rom. 8:35-38), if only we do not let go of His hand.

In fact, afflictions draw us closer to our Savior and in that sense we are victorious when to the world it seems like defeat. We can indeed say:

"Death, where is your sting?" But only through God's revealed love and grace that manifested in Yeshua (1 Cor. 15:54-57).

"He himself bore our sins" in his body on the cross, so that we might die to sin and live righteously: *"By His wounds you have been healed"* (1 Pet. 2:24 – WEB).

Frank Hanks

Empty hospitals and Frank Hanks

I have found few men as bold as Frank Hanks of emptyhospitals.org on the topic of faith healing through prayer. No, he is not a televangelist, but like many missionaries goes about his daily life, praying for those who hurt among the poor in other cultures. His book *'Training wheels'* (2013) explains how he grew in this "faith-gift operating through the Holy Spirit," as "God's methods for training His children to be miracle workers." Frank survived a life-threatening medical scare early in 2023, never wavering in his faith.

But how often are there true saint-like believers with strong faith available to pray for the sick? How many believers know how to operate not in the 'logos' Word, but to act on a 'rhema' Word; having pressed through in prayer into the Holy of Holies, into the presence of the Most High?

Most, even the very sincere and pious, lack in confidence because they have believed teachings and doctrines that made excuses for the lack of faith and the absence of miracles!

How often do we anoint the sick with oil, while calling on 'God your Healer' ('YeHoVaH Roph'ekha' or 'El Rapha'), in genuine mountain-moving faith, acting on a 'rhema' Word? (Ex. 15:26).

<u>Research confirms the memorial name of God</u>

Research lead by Dr. Nehemia Gordon, screening thousands of the most ancient Hebrew manuscripts and correspondence, has by 2022 found over 2,400 vocalizations of the memorial name of the God of Israel to be 'YeHoVaH,' with nil cases for 'Yahweh,' which seems to have originated with Gilbert Genebrard in 1699. Pietro Colonna Galatino in 1518 guessed that the Jews vocalize 'YeHoVaH' as 'Adonai,' but they say 'haShem' (literally 'the Name') when reading the tetragrammaton 'YeHoVaH.' It is pronounced 'Yehovah,' with the accent on the last syllable. The 'ye' is pronounced as 'yellow' and not as 'j' in 'jam,' as used by the JW cult. The issue is about respect and not to denigrate the name of the Almighty. See https://www.youtube.com/watch?v=dP4ogclTDto

Why allow poor theology to disarm the faithful? How often has there been a consecration of the sick? Has the dwelling been consecrated?

Is the building and environment not demon-infested and sick, or are such examples in the Old Testament in vain? Has God changed? Has the enemy changed? No!

The lack of giant-slaying faith, pure Biblical righteousness and simple practical obedience are all reasons for the absence of answered prayer for healing (2 Chr. 30:18-20).

To pray for the sick is thus both a command and an enormous challenge – for even the prayers of the Apostles sometimes failed to heal their brethren, which is why Plan A needs to be understood.

FAITH HEALING EXPLAINED

Kevin Greer

To pray is a privilege and we need to press in, for the Kingdom is taken with power, but beware of being dogmatic. Can the clay tell the potter? (Isa. 64:8; Rom. 9:21) No, we do not prescribe, but the righteous can, as in the parable of the persistent widow; ask with confidence (Luke 18:1-8).

This is what the likes of Dan Mohler, Kevin Greer, Daniel Kolenda, Franks Hanks, Mario Murillo and others who have truly seen spectacular healings will confirm: We need to find answers for the times when the 'healing stuff' does not happen the way we pray.

We need to understand the issue and ultimately grasp the fact that death is really not the 'end all' for those who have fought well, who have run the good race, who will obtain the 'crown of life' (2 Tim. 4:7-8; James 1:12).

So, what is the challenge? Are we doing the Great Commission (Mark 16:15-18), or finding excuses? Do we truly give an account of the hope of Christ in us? (Rom. 5:1-5) Do we comprehend that an account of our *"good works of faith"* will one day be demanded? (Rom. 14:12; 1 Cor. 4:1;

1 Peter 4:1-5) It is one of the basic tenets of the faith, but can we envision our responsibility?

The challenge is to overcome our fear of disappointment and timidity. Fear is a spirit that we need to confess and get out of our lives (Rom. 8:15). It is natural. Peter also had to ask for boldness to preach – and this was after Pentecost. Paul, too, asked for prayers and for boldness (Acts 14:1-31; Eph. 6:18-19).

To conclude: Faith healing through prayer is so abused, rejected and vilified because it's the most powerful and immediate way to bring the Kingdom of Heaven near to a lost world.

"As you go, preach, saying, 'The Kingdom of Heaven is at hand!' Heal the sick, cleanse the lepers, and cast out demons. Freely you received, so freely give" (Mat 10:7-8).

3. Why blunt the sword's blade?

MANY aspiring faith-healers will quote every verse in the Bible to demonstrate the ability and willingness of God to heal as Plan A, reciting healing verses in and out of context to raise the hopes and faith of the sick and suffering.

They will, however, not teach on the Biblical examples where disciples were not healed, but suffered in Christ. They do this in order not to confuse, but are using only one side of the two-edged sword until the blade is blunt.

For example: Do you hear sermons about why Paul left Trophimus sick on the island of Miletus? Or advised Timothy to drink a little wine for his ailments? (2 Tim. 4:20; 1 Tim. 5:23)

FAITH HEALING EXPLAINED

Did Paul lack faith? Did Timothy lack faith? Why don't we see any of the confidence of faith healers on display when we read Paul's letter to Philippi regarding Epaphroditus?

"Yet I considered it necessary to send to you Epaphroditus, my brother, fellow worker, and fellow soldier, but your messenger and the one who ministered to my need; since he was longing for you all, and was distressed because you had heard that he was sick.

"For indeed he was sick almost to death; but God had mercy on him, and not only on him but on me also, lest I should have sorrow upon sorrow" (Phil. 2:25-27).

It is not only, as is often presumptuously argued, about the faith of the sick believer. The sick often get unjustly blamed for a lack of faith, sin or for having demons, when healing-preachers have an over-estimation of their own integrity; which is why faith-healing must be properly understood (Mat. 7:1-5, 7:6, 7:21-23; Gal. 6:2-7).

With evangelism, healing seems to depend on grace, the faith of the preacher and a willingness of the unsaved to come to Christ, issues discussed later.

The point is that faith-healing is not just a matter of dogmatic fasting and prayer as a method of compliance. Healing doctrine must rest on *"all of Scripture"* – for the 'gift of healing' and the prayer of the righteous matter much, but utmost is the promotion of the Kingdom (1 Cor. 12:9, 28).

Healing miracles are ultimately Grace and primarily linked to the promotion of the Kingdom of God, revealing His love. Furthermore, the Holy Spirit, including the gift of healing, is NOT under the control of the pastor or prophet. *"All these [spiritual gifts] are empowered by one and the same Spirit, who apportions to each one individually as he wills"* (1 Cor. 12:11).

Most healing-preachers are men of great faith; not superior theology. A common mistake is to associate miracles with a blank cheque for having divine wisdom, and it is then that Pride and Error enter even the best of ministries.

At times saints themselves suffer illness and do not find a cure through prayer – like Paul's *"thorn"* – to discover that *"My grace is sufficient for you"* (2 Cor. 12:7-9).

Pete Greig of '24-7 Prayer,' for example, testifies of having how they were faced by a sudden and severe attack on his wife Sammy's health and though she survived, still have a battle: "The paradox of miracles on the one hand and un-miracles on the other."

Pete has discovered how his faith, through grace, has benefited from the spiritual growth of this trial.

Todd White talks about suffering the death of his grandmother with cancer and of long-term travailing prayer for children who do not get healed; "stuff" that breaks his heart, but he stays steadfast not to look for excuses, other than to admit that we are still growing to the fullness of Messiah.

Dan Mohler had to care for his bed-ridden mom for over twenty years, when he saw others with the same condition that he has prayed for healed. But her faith and graceful, saint-like demeanor in her suffering touched the hearts of all who worked with her, including those in medical practice who testified: "We have never seen one bear her cross like this."

David Yonggi Cho explained it is not simply a case of quoting Bible promises (the 'logos' Word), which can become tantamount to "abracadabra." The Word must be a Holy Spirit-inspired, a living word, 'quickened' by the Spirit, a 'rhema' Word for the situation.

FAITH HEALING EXPLAINED

<u>The gift follows unbending faith and passion</u>

The evangelists mentioned, and many others, have a passion for souls, unbending faith and seriously desire to serve the Kingdom in the capacity of this gift of the Holy Spirit. They started out by praying for people and their faith did not waver when they initially saw no results.

Many sincere saints have endured much testing in this area. There is the proverbial *"cloud of witnesses"* on earth and in heaven (Heb. 12:1), who can testify that 'the fourth person' (as with Daniel's three friends) is always with us in the furnace (Dan. 3:25).

We are indeed of more value than two sparrows: *"Are not two sparrows sold for a penny? And not one of them shall fall on the ground [in the snare] without your Father [knowing]..."* (Mat. 10:29).

As King David wrote: *"This knowledge is beyond me. It's lofty. I can't attain it. Where could I go from your Spirit? Or where could I flee from your presence?"* (Ps. 139:6-7 –WEB).

We thus see that mountain-moving faith is required in both healing, AND in sharing in the suffering of Christ. Yet, we know it is always a work of Grace; not the poison of liberal "twisted grace" (as Todd White calls it), but reverent, holy Grace: *"Grace, whereby we may serve God acceptably with reverence and godly fear: For our God is a consuming fire"* (Heb. 12:28-29).

We need both faith and obedience to pray, knowing that true love brings about transformational faith to people, always to the glory of Yeshua as King of Kings, the living Word that became flesh. Believers who get sick must hang on to their faith in Jesus; we should teach them that they can confess having 'little faith' and ask for stronger faith in prayer (Mat. 6:30). There is no shame in being honest.

4. Why miracles on the mission fields?

"JESUS [Yeshua] went about all the cities and the villages, teaching in their synagogues, and preaching the Gospel of the Kingdom, and healing every disease and every sickness among the people" (Mat. 4:23, 9:35).

Miracles occur more often on the mission fields, where the Spirit mightily confirms the preaching of the Gospel and brings light to those in darkness. The desperation of the poor and the lack of medical facilities add to the urgency to press in with prayer.

This explains why 'sold out for Jesus' evangelists and missionaries, being more fully developed in their Christ-likeness, testify of countless miracles where they take the Gospel to 'virgin soil' — to multitudes bound in darkness. When the Light of the Word goes to areas where the message of salvation is new; places where the basic Gospel is preached and believed with childlike faith.

Many times a 'word of knowledge' is received regarding the health of a person (1 Cor. 12:8), following which the faith-prayer by the missionary/ evangelist results in healing, faith and full conversion. It is the Holy Spirit that does the work, the same power that resurrected Christ, always pointing to our King and not to the one who prayed.

Actually, the big question is this: How much is it bold prayer and how much a special spiritual gift or anointment resting on the evangelist, missionary or pastor? (1 Cor. 12:9-28).

Daniel Kolenda, who inherited the baton from Reinhard Bonnke as leader of 'Christ for all Nations' in 2009, in May 2023 lead a huge team of Cfan evangelists on a record-breaking mass evangelistic campaign in Zambia, preaching simultaneously for five days in each of 11 different cities over a period of two weeks.

FAITH HEALING EXPLAINED

Daniel Kolenda, Cfan

The 55 meetings recorded over 2.6 million in attendance and 1,040,720 signed "decisions for Jesus Christ." This brought the total for Cfan up to over 88 million decisions since Bonnke started in 1967.

What Kolenda and Western evangelists surely need to be aware of, is the temptation /motivation for local pastors to "assist in miracles happening," hoping that their congregations will multiply tenfold. The motive in such cases is the same as that of fake healers who convince themselves that "it's for the good, it's for the Gospel, it is to promote the Kingdom," and so on.

As stated before, man's heart is very deceptive. It could explain why one would see tens of thousands of people, especially in heavily populated, immensely poor and undeveloped areas, out of curiosity, flock to these huge crusades. Then, emotionally encouraged, they "make decisions for Christ," but, as in the parable of the sower, much of the seed always falls on the rocky places, among the weed and so on (Luke 8:5-8).

Revivals (where the Gospel is known but neglected) and Crusades (among people where Christ is largely unknown) do not equal an

Awakening. Contrary to a true Awakening, it does not visibly or immediately change the morality of a city or country. With an Awakening, the impact is immense and immediate. It changes culture and has an effect on several generations.

The famous David Yonggi Cho of Yoido Full Gospel Church in Seoul tells of how, at the start of his career in the late 1950's, he struggled to garner the boldness of faith to hold a healing-meeting for his severely impoverished church members.

Speaking at Paradise, Australia in 1983 (I viewed it on *YouTube* in April 2016), he recalled how tormented he was in his faith beforehand, hoping that only those with non-visible ailments such as flu or stomach pains would come forward, but he was challenged to pray for two deaf girls!

Yonggi Cho (1936-2021)

Yonngi told of how he struggled to take his hands from the first girl's ears, fearing to find no result. God was gracious and confirmed his servant's prayer and so started a mighty ministry that has affected the Kingdom. He operated with the Holy Spirit's unction and by simply following the instructions in the Word of God, knowing that the presence of the 'Comforter' is like having Jesus with us in our endeavors for His Kingdom.

FAITH HEALING EXPLAINED

People, of course, want healing, but there is no formula or human logic. It is by grace and a work of the Spirit. So, we should pray knowing that the results do not depend on us, but on the Holy Spirit, for *"the power of the Lord for healing is present"* (Luke 5:17).

Do so with faith and confidence. It is amazing to see how a very simple prayer in the name of Jesus, but filled with great faith, can result in healing. Be careful about claims of being a 'faith-healer' when prayer is answered. The testimony should always point the glory to our King.

These 'faith-healers' know how to press in with prayer. Their prayers are brief, but powerful, and if there is no result at first, they continue to pray again and again, knowing that faith does not accept defeat when the Spirit's unction inspires.

Those are times when believers should not surrender when results do not seem to be immediately forthcoming, for sometimes mountains move in small steps and we should press in with the divine authority of Him who binds *"the Pleiades, or loosen the cords of Orion"* (Job 38:31).

This is Biblical – take the case of when Yeshua healed the blind man in Bethsaida and he at first could only see *"people walking like trees"* (Mark 8:22-26). Doing it as an example, He then continued to pray and the man's sight was fully restored.

Todd White, who famously followed the example of his mentor Dan Mohler, prayed for about one thousand people (on average ten a day) over six months before he saw his first miracle.

Mohler himself, working as a storeman after being freshly re-birthed and "on fire for Jesus," was mocked by colleagues, but persisted to pray for healing whenever he found someone hurting. Then, one day at work, he suddenly received a 'word of knowledge' about the medical condition of a truck driver and the back of a complete stranger got healed. Faith grows with such results and the Kingdom advances.

5. How do we judge the use of gifts?

OPEN the newspapers in South Africa, Nigeria and some other countries and see how many faith-healers, boasting with the titles of 'prophet,' 'bishop,' 'apostle' and even the odd 'prophet professor,' have descended on the flock, ravaging the Bride-to-be (Rev. 21:2-10); damaging the reputation of the faithful among the ordained brethren.

One attribute of God (YeHoVaH) is that He is jealous ('El Kanno' – Ex. 20:5). Why focus on the preacher if the healing is divine? There is a fine line between having a testimony and to advertise healing for the promotion of a career.

Those in 'less developed' societies often find them in the hands of the 'traditional healers' of their cultures: the 'sangomas' and 'shamans.' Whatever the culture or situation, healing is expensive and attracts a wide variety of professionals, real and fake, as it has been from Biblical times. *"A woman who had a flow of blood for twelve years, who had spent all her living on physicians, and could not be healed by any came behind Him [Yeshua], and touched the fringe of his cloak, and immediately the flow of her blood stopped"* (Luke 8:43-44).

The sporadic 'angel's stirring the water' at the Bath of Bethesda mentioned in John 5 was typical of an intermittent spring, similar to the famous Gihon Spring. The news that Yeshua had healed a man at the bath caused a huge 'stir' among the religious powers.

A man who was born blind similarly challenged the temple rulers regarding Yeshua — that His healing power pointed to one fact only — that He had to be the Messiah. This presented a massive challenge to the Sadducees and Pharisees and encouraged them to murder Him at the time of Passover.

Nothing has changed: Yeshua still presents a huge challenge to all false faith systems and also to the Church in its response to healings and miracles (Mark 16:17-18). Ordinary believers are challenged to overcome fear of the 'opinions of men' and become genuine disciples (John 12:43; Gal. 1:10).

As Spurgeon once said: "The fear of God is the death of every other fear; like a mighty lion, it chases away all other fears." We need to pray and ask for the gift of the Holy Spirit and then, in faith, go out to the harvest fields. We are in the post-Pentecost era of the Great Commission, are we not?

The great evangelist Reinhard Bonnke used to say: "The traffic light is green, it says Go! But don't follow a parked car to get somewhere – also do not follow a 'parked pastor.'" Derek Prince (1915-2003) shared similar farmer's logic: "Don't put a new chick under a dead hen!"

The fact that Yeshua did not comment on the (seemingly) mysterious healings at the Bath of Bethesda holds a very important lesson for the ministries of others – even those dubious, bling-loving faith-healers. Seek truth and protect the flock, but leave the judgment of religious charlatans to God!

"Therefore judge nothing before the time, until the Master comes, who will both bring to light the hidden things of darkness, and reveal the counsels of the hearts. Then each man will get his praise from God" (1 Cor. 3:5). People self-judge themselves by what they say, do and also with doctrinal-unbelief: *"And judge yourselves unworthy of everlasting life"* (Acts 13:46).

We have a duty not to judge by mere appearances, but to judge correctly (John 17:24); to have wisdom in how we reason and in how we try to correct others, remembering not to *"give that which is holy to the dogs"*

(Mat. 7:6). We are to focus on our primary mission, which is to represent our King-Messiah.

Note that the Bath of Bethesda was at the sheep market – Yeshua's flock knows His voice; He is the Gate to 'the Narrow Way' so many do not find (John 5:2): *"This is the gate of YeHoVaH, through which the righteous shall enter"; "Because strait is the gate, and narrow is the way, which leads to life, and few find it"; "Yeshua said to him, I am the way, the truth, and the life: no man comes to the Father, but by me"* (Ps. 118:20; Mat. 7:14; John 14:5).

Prayer warriors must understand that the focus is not so much on engaging in a battle with demons, but to pray for the flock to stay in the Word, to walk in truth, the Holy Spirit always pointing towards Messiah, for the Gospel is guided by *"the Spirit of Jesus"* (Acts 16:7 – NIV, also the Vulgate Latin, Syriac and Ethiopic versions).

"Do not speak evil of one another, brethren. He who speaks evil of a brother and judges his brother, speaks evil of the law and judges the law. But if you judge the law, you are not a doer of the law but a judge" (James 4:1).

It's often not understood that the gifts of the Spirit are irrevocable (Rom. 11:29); David understood that King Saul remained God's anointed despite his backsliding. A faith healer who has lost his or her way can still have the faith and the spiritual gift for healing, but it does not mean that he or she is operating in the full truth of the Gospel!

A faith-healer who has fallen in love with fame and bling still has the gift. The fact that he continues to operate in ministry serves as a test and is not an indication that he is preaching or living the truth of the Gospel (1 Kings 13's lesson)!

Deceptive spirits are sent to test believers – as the early Church was repeatedly warned. Those who so firmly believe that they cannot be misled by deceiving spirits, assuming all their spiritual experiences to be divine, are probably already deceived.

Today's prayer warriors and their 'decrees,' claiming victory before the race has been completed, remind one of the Jews who recited promises to the patriarchs and 'decreed' that Jerusalem could never fall because God's temple was there.

A sure sign of being under the influence of bad teaching is when ordinary believers become uncorrectable and arrogant: *"For the time will come when they will not listen to the sound doctrine, but, having itching ears, will heap up for themselves teachers after their own lusts"* (2 Tim. 4:3).

6. What if a dark place is God's plan?

TROUBLE is sometimes part of the redemption plan. The classic example was when Moses went to Pharaoh to let Israel go and the Egyptian slave drivers responded by making life even harder. *"O Lord [Adonai] why have you brought trouble on this people? ...You have not rescued your people at all,"* Moses cried, not knowing of the calamities and drama that waited on them (Exo. 5:22-23).

Many believers are in a dark place with their health, be it due to age, the ravages of corruption and the decay of our flesh. Even worse are those who are still young and suffer illness because of, or a mysterious cause, an accident, or inherited.

And then there is the taboo in modern society to dare mention dark family sins manifesting as per the Ten Commandments: *"visiting the iniquity of the fathers on the children to the third and fourth generation of those who hate me"* (Exo. 34:7 Deu. 5:9).

Jesus did not ascribe the collapse of the Tower of Siloam in Jerusalem, killing eighteen (Luke 13:4), on the devil. We must not credit the enemy for everything?!

But even if disease and disaster are the work of our mortal enemy, the devil prowls like *"a roaring lion,"* or came because of the 'Law of Sin,' so what? The evil one's days are limited. He knows he is due to be bound soon and the power of death, as the last enemy, will be broken. We have the promise and assurance of this in the resurrection victory of our Messiah (1 Peter 5:8).

However, if people have spent a lifetime in Egypt, why be surprised if the diseases of Egypt come on them? Having spent a lifetime of devouring un-kosher stuff, why think a sudden New Age-detox diet will work miracles when cancer or other diseases manifest? (Deu. 28:27, 35, 60).

What we need to know is that life is short, even for us who by grace have been re-birthed in spirit, for we are all on borrowed time, as Paul explained: *"For we know that if our earthly house, this tent [your weak body], is destroyed, we have a building from God, a house not made with hands [an eternal spiritual body after the resurrection], eternal in the heaven"* (2 Cor. 5:1).

The difference between those who are healthy at present and those in the last phases of life is just in the length of *"the silver cord"* (Ecc. 12:6).

Are many not perhaps in a dark place because our health is of much less consequence than the eternal destiny of our souls? There are a multitude of causes of disease, but there is only one cure for the restoration of life to the soul. That man must meet with the only One who has defeated death, Yeshua, our Messiah.

There are numerous examples in the history of Israel where calamity and sickness resulted from their sins and we did not see Elijah or Elisha intervene, because they understood that repentance does not come at the placid pools of prosperity, nor in the wards of self-pity, worldly regret and remorse.

It is often only when people find them in a 'dark place' – be it in your soul, your marriage, your health, or your poverty – that people in desperation reach out to Jesus and the germination of faith-seed can take place. A season of pruning is needed to produce good fruit.

Real repentance, resulting in transformation, usually starts in a 'dark place.' For 'teshuva,' repentance, is a gift of life: *"For godly sorrow produces repentance to salvation, which brings no regret. But the sorrow of the world produces death" (2 Cor. 7:10).*

Faced with so many requests to pray for sick people, believers must consider the deeper reason for people falling sick. Are many not perhaps in a dark place with their health – be it physical or mental – because a fire has been lit, like under a pot full of lead or silver, to separate the dross from the metal?

Is it not our nature to think that we are okay in our faith? And the healthy are vigorous in their own esteem? That our theology is good and that our souls are 'okay'?

Does the dark place, in our response to it, not perhaps have the potential to remove impurity from souls? Does the attack on our health not turn into favor when it brings us to a dark place where the only Light is Yeshua? Is a dark place not often the only way of meeting with the only real Healer, our Messiah? (Prov. 25:4; Isa. 1:25).

Millions, however, suffer the consequences of being captives of pagan culture, both old or new, held in bondage by a mindset in conflict with their Creator.

Teaching, correction and reproof are hence sorely needed (2 Tim. 3:16), which starts with prayer for a genuine desire to conform the intellect to

God's truth and His Word, to quote Nancy Pearcey, author of 'The Toxic War on Masculinity.'

Why do we say Yeshua defeated death and yet billions are in the valley of death and will feel the Grim Reaper's sickle and taste the bitter realization that they have run out of time? (Job 10:21-22; Joel 3:14). Death, as the 'last enemy,' is the one great reality and the one great leveler of men, regardless of their faith or opinion, but its power is only until the General Resurrection (1 Cor. 15:12-29).

Because of the 'double jeopardy principle,' those who through rebirth are *"in Christ"* will not taste the second death, for a sin cannot be punished twice, and Jesus has already paid the price (Rom. 8:1; Rev. 2:11, 20:6, 14). What is required is for us to believe AND obey: *"Go and sin no more"* (John 8:11); *"For all have sinned, and come short of the glory of God"* (Rom. 3:23).

Regarding the millions who, seemingly, have not had a fair chance to respond to the Gospel – a question often raised by unbelievers – ignorance is no excuse, for creation and all of nature are evidence of His goodness (Lev. 4:22, 27; Acts 14:15-18).

"God has not left himself without a testimony, for when Gentiles, who do not have the law, by nature do the things in the law, these, although not having the law, are a law to themselves, who show the work of the law written in their hearts, their conscience also bearing witness" (Rom. 2:14-16).

This principle is seen with Chief Abimelech, a great example of God's grace and righteousness, who in his innocence took Sarah into his harem: *"And God said to him in a dream, "Yes, I know you did this in the integrity of your heart. For I also withheld you from sinning against Me; therefore, I did not let you touch her"* (Gen. 20:6)

But see the blank expression on the face of so many when we mention the second death. At funerals, Revelation 21:4 is often quoted for consolation, but never verse 8: *"And God will wipe away every tear from their eyes; there shall be no more death, nor sorrow, nor crying. There shall be no more pain, for the former things have passed away... But for the fearful, and unbelieving, and abominable, and murderers, and fornicators, and sorcerers, and idolaters, and all liars, their part [shall be] in the lake that burns with fire and brimstone; which is the second death"* (Rev. 21:4, 8).

Okay, so most of us are not 'whoremongers, murderers or sorcerers,' but qualify for having been fearful or unbelieving, dishonest or of having the modern idols of money, bling and stuff; also the idols of sport, entertainment, food and the flesh, not so?

By the way, where in the Bible is a hint of dead liars being prayed out of purgatory? There was no such promise for the unbelieving robber on the cross (Luke 23:39-43).

Heaven is not overpopulated; the 'RIP' on many gravestones is a lie – there is no peace for the wicked (Isa. 48:22, 57:21). There is no 'RIP Charlie Hebdo,' for liberal blasphemers – nor for those who misinterpret grace; for truly there is only a single road that leads to heaven and it is straight and narrow, not crooked and wide. If there was an easier way, why was it required from Christ to go to the Cross? Did Yeshua not say that few shall find the 'Narrow Way'? (Mat 7:4).

'RIP Charlie Hebdo'

The terror attack on this French satirical weekly in January 2015 raised international protest and concern for liberal 'freedom of speech.' The cartoon, famed for its gross vulgarity and regular blasphemy, ignited a Phinehas-type of response from two Muslim men (Num. 25:7-13).

7. What do we learn from Wigglesworth?

LET us examine the testimony of the renowned evangelist Smith Wigglesworth (1859-1947) and see how the gift of healing gradually and famously developed in his ministry and see how it is functioning in these days.

May it inspire believers that Plan A prayer by the righteous always 'avails much' (James 5:16), and not to allow the devil of poor doctrine and small faith to fence in the operation of the Holy Spirit. Remember the poverty of Nazareth for not believing (Mat. 13:54-58). Do not, however, mistake mystic spiritualism for the functioning of the Holy Spirit (Luke 9:55).

Smith Wigglesworth (1859-1947)

Wigglesworth held the honorable title of 'brother' and there is much to learn from how he progressed from rebirth at the age of seven, to eventually being anointed by the Spirit and speaking in tongues only forty years later! (Yes, many who read this will roll their eyes and sigh. My reply to them is that eventually even Lazarus heard 'the Voice' penetrate the walls of his grave!)

Wigglesworth had a Christ-like passion for the poor and suffering from a very young age and experienced an anointing of the Holy Spirit with his confirmation at the age of about ten or eleven, when an old Episcopal bishop laid hands on him. He was surprised to see that the other boys who were 'confirmed' together with him continued unchanged, swearing and being naughty.

The first prayer for healing by the Wigglesworth couple was when their children had the flu. He took poor sick people to faith-healing meetings in a nearby town, but one day was requested to take the pulpit in the pastor's absence.

No one was more surprised than Wigglesworth to see all twelve sick people at the meeting healed, which gave him the confidence to start healing meetings in his hometown. And so did his famous healing ministry start, long before his anointment with the Holy Spirit at the age of 47 (Mat. 3:11).

As his healing ministry grew in strength of faith, Wigglesworth suddenly came down with a severe case of advanced appendicitis. Two fellow tongue-speaking, mountain-moving believers came to his house and, under inspiration of the Spirit, summoned a demon from a very surprised Wigglesworth, resulting in his instant healing.

By the time the doctor returned on his 'house-call' – fearing the worst for his patient – he found Smith has indeed departed, but to work, not the afterlife!

Prayer for healing does not exclude seeking natural remedy: Faith in the supernatural does not exclude healing in the natural. We thank our heavenly father in Yeshua's name for healing in whatever way it is provided – be it through miracle, or by medical science and procedures. The wisdom and technological advances in the provision of health care facilities are grace and not a curse; the absence of health care in nations is darkness prevailing.

This testimony of arguably the best-known Pentecostal faith-healer of the 20th century is very important: being fresh from his baptism with the Holy Spirit, Wigglesworth had no connection with the occult except from the hazard of driving them out.

Many born-again believers view themselves as immune against demonic attack and erroneously think that long-term disease is only because of inferior faith, but it is a spoken curse that will not avail (Numbers 23:8; Prov. 26:2), being re-birthed in the spirit does not provide immunity for the flesh. Our bodies are still frail, suffering aging and can be attacked by demon and virus alike; wisdom is needed in dealing with serpent and poison (Mark 16:18).

The enemy never sleeps; the 'roaring lion' still prowls the streets (1 Peter 5:8). Be Jude 1:8-complaint; be on guard against deception (Mat. 7:15, 21-22; 2 Cor. 11:3-4; 2 Tim. 4:3), and also avoid sons-of-Skeva-like bravado (Acts 19:16; Jude 1:9).

Note that water baptism drives ill-spirits to the surface and the demonic needs to be decisively dealt with: It is not a circus, it is not for entertainment as one see on some TV channels – why push a camera into the face of someone wriggling and ranting with a demon?! Does the same not go for healings? Testimonies are to the glory of the Kingdom, not the 'ministry'!

As a sidenote: Wigglesworth was known for his great faith and boldness when praying for healing, but during his global tour in 1936, he stayed with David du Plessis, the General Secretary of the Pentecostal Movement in Johannesburg at the time. Early one morning, Wigglesworth summoned the driver to take him twelve miles (19 km) to the office of Du Plessis, who used to start work at sunrise.

The burly old evangelist burst into Du Plessis' office, rammed him up the wall, looked him in the eye and delivered a powerful prophecy. An hour later, Wigglesworth again returned, very placid.

When asked about the brashness of his delivery, the old saint reminded Du Plessis about the urgency when delivering a prophetic word, of not wasting time on greetings as in the example in 1 Kings 13 of a prophet that got killed by a lion for disobeying the instruction.

The short-term part of the prophecy to Du Plessis was that he would travel the world (which he did) and the long-term part foretold of three revivals, of which the last will be the greatest and will predominantly happen among traditional churches!

What we pray and how we pray obviously matters, which in turn clearly depends on what we believe, making ecclesiology important. The word 'revival' is often abused with bogus claims of works by the 'Holy Spirit,' which is why believers must urgently study the Word independently and with more fervor and prayer for insight to discern the real from the counterfeit. To be strengthen us for the coming separation of the sheep from the goats (Mat. 25:32-33).

We are not at 'The End-of-the-world,' as many fear, but and the 'End-of-an-Age,' the 'two days' Hosea 6:2 speaks of, which must be read with Luke 21:24: *"and Jerusalem will be trampled underfoot by the Gentiles, until the times of the Gentiles are fulfilled."*

We or our children could be the generation to see both the Great Awakening and the gathering 'of the dead bones of Israel' (Eze. 37:1-14), when the Ark will not even be mentioned, a gathering of fame equal to the miracle of the Exodus (Jer. 3:14-22; 23:3-8).

8. Have we really done all we can?

"IS any sick among you? Let him call for the elders of the church [ecclesia]; and let them pray over him, anointing him with oil ['shemen'] in the name ['shem'] of the Lord" (James 5:14)

The anointment with oil was part of the daily beauty regime of people in ancient times. It was also specifically practiced with the inauguration of the High Priest, kings and with burials. Remember how Jesus was anointed in advance for his burial (Mat. 26:7-9).

James 5 confirms this practice to be part of Plan A-prayers. There is more to anointment oil than what we understand. Some faith-healers use olive oil mixed with frankincense, which was always presented with burned sacrifices as *"a sweet savour to YeHoVaH"* (Lev. 2:1-2). Frankincense and myrrh were presented as gifts to the parents of Yeshua. Myrrh, cinnamon and calamus are mentioned as the *"three principal spices"* (Ex. 30:23), while Psalm 45:8 mentions garments smelling of myrrh, aloes and cassia *"make you glad."*

There are, however, three aspects that are possibly missed in the application of the traditional 'Anointment of the Sick' sacrament as it is practiced in some churches:

The first aspect is 'the Name': *"Thy name is as ointment poured forth,"* declares Song of Solomon 1:3. The blessing is where oil is applied 'in the Name' – a therapy lost in the sterility of faith in modern medicine, as our Healers' memorial Name has also been lost (Ex. 3:13), but now affirmed, *"I will make my holy name known among my people Israel"* (Eze. 39:7).

Calling the elders is the second very important but often missed aspect, especially among believers who are not affiliated with an assembly. The third aspect is fasting, as discussed in Book 2.

FAITH HEALING EXPLAINED

We need to realize that 'the Name' is *"beyond comprehension,"* as the parents of Samson were told (Jdg. 13:17-21); secondly that all authority in heaven and earth rests in our King Messiah (Mat. 28:18).

There is thus more involved than the correct pronunciation of 'the Name' and the conjuration thereof as found among 'Sacred Name' eccentrics – it is about the total integrity of our relationship with Yeshua and the presence of the 'Comforter.' That said, this anointment prayer can be done by calling on God our Healer as 'YeHoVaH Rapha' (Ps. 68:4; Isa. 26:4), always asking in the name of Yeshua.

The traditional response has been to fast and pray; to call on the brethren to join in prayer; to request a visit by the elders (righteous believers with a proven walk of deep faith); to anoint the sick while calling on the Name of our Healer. Then, depending on the prompting of the Holy Spirit, to cast out and bind demonic spirits: Be it unrepentance, fear, bitterness, unforgiveness and so on.

Is the very act of obedience, the gathering the elders and anointing the sick, not in itself a good testimony of faith in our Healer, despite the condition of the flesh? Is compassionate prayer not a visible sign of His love in us?

When there is no immediate visible healing, we should never give up, but persist and continue to press in, again and again. Should, however, all our efforts over a long time seem to go unanswered, we should not ignore such cases and, as some 'healing-teachers' do. There is no need to hide those apparent 'failures,' but seek God's face ['panav YeHoVaH Yeshua'] for answers, for Plan A is all-encompassing.

Has the possibility of a demonic attack been addressed and the common problem of an incomplete spiritual rebirth considered?

What pet sin is being pampered, and what false doctrine is being propagated? Not that it affects the integrity of the saint, doing the prayer of healing; God does not use an enemy-attack to "teach us lessons," but do we teach healing when truth calls for repentance? Or profess grace when heaven calls for confession?

This is why prayer in the Spirit ['tongues'] is so vital: To pray according to the will of the Almighty and not our instinctive human desire and logic, trusting for the Holy Spirit to inspire, always asking in the name of Yeshua (1 Cor. 14:1-40).

We should teach about grace, but also about being obedient to the Gospel. We should never let little faith, poor doctrines and ignorance on this subject undermine the operation of the Holy Spirit, even when there is no visible miracle (1 Cor. 12:9-31).

What do we do when healing does not manifest, and a beloved is near the exit door of this temporary life?

Several years ago, a Torah-observant Messianic friend of ours passed away after the typical battle against cancer. She was a fever-ravaged skeleton of her former self, yet her good husband still 'professed healing' in her last days: "Lovey, you are healed in the name of Yeshua, take your healing," etcetera.

Why did they prolong her misery? Only a day before her departure did they find the wisdom and faith to release her to go in peace.

At the risk to oversimply the debate, the following questions need to be considered:

One: When does prayer become a 'mantra'? The hope that if spoken often enough, it will come to fruition? Scriptures should never be quoted habitually.

Two: Why expect a miracle, but disrespect Yeshua as the Word of God, interpreting the Bible as they wish? *"Those who are in the flesh can't please God"* (John 1:1-14; Rom. 8:8; Rev. 1:2).

Three: Is there respect towards other members of the 'body of Christ'? Is there respect for the way the 'cup and bread' is shared? It could be a major reason for causing believers to be *"weak and sick and a number of you have fallen away"* (1 Cor. 11:17-30).

Four: Comprehension of everlasting life is not professed by such desperation. Such behavior undervalues the Glory of Heaven for those who truly are 'in Christ.' Why expect a Pentecostal-miracle but deny the full scope of the Gospel's truth regarding who Yeshua was and is?

Many Christians are in a similar position, being in churches where doctrine (like the 'chains of Calvin') limits Pentecostal-faith for the operation of the Holy Spirit, including healing. They have faith in God, but not in the full teachings of the Gospel. They are like Apollos of Alexandria, who was mighty in the Scriptures, yet had to be explained 'The Way' more accurately (Acts 18:26). Yeshua did not heal many in Nazareth not because of His ability, but because of their rejection of Him (Mark 6:5-6).

9. When God says "enough!"

"ENOUGH!" is what the Almighty told Moses when he pleaded to enter the Promised Land. He was old, a 120 years, but not frail and still had good eyesight and was not keen on leaving this world – so Moses implored or begged God to change the earlier decree against him and his brother Aaron (Num. 20:8-12, 27:12-14; Deu. 3:26).

'Enough!' is also what Paul was told after he prayed a third time to be healed from his embarrassing illness: *"A thorn in the flesh was given to me, a messenger of Satan to buffet me, lest I be exalted above measure"* (2 Cor. 12:7).

'Enough!' is thus often the reply from God in answer to the fervent prayers of the sick and suffering when it's time to depart. But unlike Moses and Paul, people praying desperately for a loved one not to die usually don't hear the answer, for silence is also an answer.

Imagine the magnitude of prayers so many millions of terminally ill have prayed over the centuries, yet they have all returned to dust.

The prophet Isaiah went to King Hezekiah to tell him he must prepare to die. The king then petitioned God on the grounds of his good works, and the answer came even before Jeremiah had left the palace (2 Kings 20:4).

An important fact about this famous healing is usually overlooked: It meant an extension of fifteen years to the Kingdom of Judah before the first destruction of Jerusalem... at the predestined date. Much more was thus at stake than king Hezekiah's life — it was a covenant and Kingdom matter!

I believe that the same reason applies to all other divine healing interventions in the lives of men: It's always about covenant and the promotion of the Kingdom of God. Otherwise, God would be unfair, and that is not possible, is it? I'm sure there's no giant lucky draw lotto wheel in heaven to decide whose prayers should be answered and who's not.

However, fifteen years later, Hezekiah passed on, having done only foolishly in the extension of his lifespan. So, when one's days are finished, when the task and journey have been completed, then eventually the answer will be: 'Enough!'

FAITH HEALING EXPLAINED

"Prayer is one of the best preparations for death,' Matthew Henry (1662-1714), wrote three centuries ago in his famous commentary on the Bible about 2 Kings 20:1-1: "A warning to prepare for death was brought to king Hezekiah by Isaiah, because by it (such a message) we fetch strength and grace from God, to enable us to finish well.

"The king wept sorely: hence some may gather that he was unwilling to die; it's in the nature of man to dread the separation of soul and body... Hezekiah's piety made his sick-bed prayer easy: He did not speak as if God needed to be reminded of anything; nor, as if a reward might be demanded; It's Christ's righteousness only that is the purchase of mercy and grace. Hezekiah did not pray: "Lord, Lord, spare me," but he said, "Remember me; whether I live or die, let me be thine."

"It is our duty, when sick, to use such means as are proper to help nature (healing), else we do not trust God, but tempt Him. For the confirmation of Hezekiah's faith, the shadow on the sundial was miraculously extended... This wonder showed the power of God in heaven and on earth, the great notice He takes of prayer and the great favor He bears to His chosen."

For God has already provided a way – 'the Way' in Yeshua, our Blessed Assurance: *"Beloved, if our hearts don't condemn us, we have boldness toward God; and whatever we ask, we receive from him, because we keep his commandments and do the things that are pleasing in his sight"* (1 John 3:21-22)

With Creation, the Almighty had already foreseen both the mortality of the first Adam, and the immortality of the second Adam in Christ, in Yeshua appearing in the flesh (1 Cor. 15:20-26).

Both the 1st and Last Adam were uniquely created from one part dust and one part breath of God ('Ruach'). Both came with absolute dominion, both were tempted, both sacrificed, but the one's son sacrificed a lamb, the other Son Himself as the Lamb as we see in (Gen. 4:4; John 19:30-37).

A second step in the healing process is often missed. If healing is step one, then restoration is step two (Numbers 12:13-14). *"Go show you to the priest,"* was the instruction to lepers in Matthew 8:4 and Luke 17:14, as per the 'Law of Leprosy' in Leviticus 13 and 14.

Yes, healing preachers operate under the New Covenant, but if they quote Moses on healing, tithing and positive prophecies related only to Israel, why hesitate to accept God's other guidelines for the health and welfare of His people?

For example, In Judaism, the 'mikveh' bath plays the role of purification and restoration after sickness and impurity, but is there any similar process in Christianity? If prayer for healing is like 'rolling away the stone from the grave,' what then equals the 'loosening of the bandages of Lazarus'? (John 11:44). How many people who come close to death, and then with the aid of prayer, grace and/or medical science recover, but then just continue with their old lifestyles?

The 'mikveh' calendar

Rivkah Bloom's MikvahCalendar.com is a great source for all females, not only Jewish women regarding 'family purity' and health in observing a monthly abstinence. ('Mikveh' is modern Hebrew, some still use 'mikvah.')

Victory over terminal illness sometimes comes as in the case Hezekiah's miraculous healing as either a Kingdom-matter or a testimony, but eventually Hezekiah, and Lazarus too, passed on in the natural. Sickness is terminal only to the flesh; not the soul and spirit of believers.

Take the case of the ten lepers in Samaria we read about in Luke 17: *"So when He saw them, He said to them, "Go, show you to the priests."* And so it was that as they went, they were cleansed, and one of them, when he saw he was healed, returned, and with a loud voice glorified God, and fell down on his face at His feet, giving Him thanks. And he was a Samaritan.

"So Jesus answered and said, "Were there not ten cleansed? But where are the nine? "Were there not any found who returned to give glory to God except this foreigner?" And He said to him, "Arise, go your way. Your faith has made you well [saved you]..." (Luke 17:11-19).

Ten were thus healed, but only one got saved. The flesh is a temporary matter; far more important is faith that makes the soul well and rebirths the spirit.

Sickness and obedience go back to Israel's deliverance and the test at the bitter waters of Mara.

"If you diligently heed the voice of YeHoVaH your God and do what is right in His sight, give ear to His commandments and keep all His statutes, I will put none of the diseases on you which I have brought on the Egyptians. For I am YeHoVaH who heals you..." (Ex. 15:26-27).

"For anyone who eats and drinks without discerning the body, eats and drinks judgment on himself. That is why many of you are weak and ill, and some have died. But if we judged ourselves truly, we would not be judged." (1 Cor. 11:27-31).

The Great Mystery

1 Timothy 3:16: "And without controversy great is the mystery of godliness: God was manifest in the flesh, justified in the Spirit, seen of angels, preached to the Gentiles, believed on in the world, received up into glory."

Does the world not doubt the credentials of a 'loving God' every time there is a disaster or a child dies? Do most people not expect God to be a benevolent old Caretaker, the 'Ancient of Days'? (Daniel 7:9).

Is it not one reason why people struggle so much with the Old Testament, preferring to hear only about a God that *"so loved the world,"* John 3:16, but ignoring 3:18 and 3:36, for example?

It's important for the terminally ill, but also their families, to understand that it is simply the natural way for all flesh. This is what the elderly – if wise and believing – get to realize when old age destroys the vanity of beauty; when the fleeting passage of time prepares the soul to part from its frame of dust.

Paul explained this well when he too lamented the temporary nature of life: *"For we know that if our earthly house, this tent, is destroyed, we have a building from God, a house not made with hands, eternal in the heavens..."* (2 Cor. 5:1).

<u>Why call the Almighty the 'Ancient of days'?</u>

The word 'ancient' points to 'everlasting' (Dan. 9: 13, 22; Ps. 90:2; Isa. 9:6). The Almighty Creator [YeHoVaH] is outside of time, space and matter. God was unified with the Voice and Spirit from the very beginning, placing the triune God beyond the realm of the 'Big Bang' theory (Gen. 1:1-3). It is for this reason that Isaiah 9 mentions 'Almighty Father' as one title ascribed to Yeshua; being the Voice and Image of Father and the First of Creation: *"And His name shall be called Wonderful, Counselor, Mighty God, Everlasting Father, Prince of Peace"* (Isa. 9:6).

So, this is then not a chapter on false promises, but to explain why the answer to the prayers of the righteous is sometimes answered by silence or by God saying, "Enough!" when its time for our promotion to glory as the old folks used to say.

Never wait for the last day to get done what you have been called for. We all have this ONE life to prepare for life everlasting.

May we be counted worthy to be called "good servants" of our King! *"Well done, good and faithful servant. You have been faithful over a little; I will set you over much. Enter into the joy of your master"* (Mat. 25:21).

10. Do we share a paranoia about death?

"IT is in the nature of man to dread the separation of soul and body," (Matthew Henry's commentary), but as believers, we do not share the paranoia of the world about death. This is true in times of war and great calamity, but also when ordinary people face death.

"But I would not have you ignorant, brothers, concerning those who are asleep, that you be not grieved, even as others who have no hope" (1 The. 4:13). Yeshua, referring to the deceased body of his friend, said: *"Lazarus sleeps,"* fully confirming that the Almighty is *"not the God of the dead, but the God of the living: you therefore do greatly err"* (John 11:11; Mark 23:27).

"It was very common among the Jews to express death by sleep; and expressions such a 'falling asleep,' 'sleeping with their fathers,' etc., were in great use among them. The Hebrews probably used this form of speech to signify their belief in the soul's immortality and the resurrection of the body." – Adam Clarke (1762-1832) remarked.

When Stephen was martyred, he forgave, kneeled down and *"went to sleep"* (Acts 7:60). It does not mean that we do not mourn loved ones; in that we have the example in John 11:33: *"When Jesus saw her crying, and the Jews who were crying with her, he was deeply moved and troubled."*

To put our sadness second to our relationship with Father – through Yeshua – is embodied in the 'Shabbat hi mi-lizok' principle – 'on Sabbath we do not cry.' It dates from the time the returned Exiles gathered in Jerusalem and were taught the Law: *"Today is holy to YeHoVaH your God. Don't mourn, nor weep." For all the people wept when they heard the words of the law..."* (Neh. 8:9).

It is also the principle of the 'Kaddish,' the Aramaic prayer said by mourners and with the Yom Kippur service. Those who pray acknowledge that God is in control and that—even as we grieve over the death of a loved one—we know the Almighty is the Giver of life.

If God had to obey people's pleas regarding death, very few souls would ever have passed on! As said, in the case of non-terminal ailments, the example of Paul was to pray three times for healing and then to accept His will (2 Cor. 12:8), unless prompted by the Spirit to press home in faith and expect healing.

This has nothing to do with little faith – Paul surely cannot be blamed for small faith! It has to do with having 'fear of God' ['yirad Yah'], being in awe of the Creator God, which means to have holy respect for His divine will (Ps. 19:9).

The secret of not sharing the world's paranoia regarding death is a firm conviction that our mortality has been defeated at the grave. Illness is buried with our corruptible flesh, for in Christ the victory has been secured at the Cross. When our time on earth is completed, life goes on in the next glorious dimension of Spirit. The flesh waits for the day of the Great Trumpet for redemption (1 Cor. 15:52).

This we also see when Moses had to accept that God's grace is more than what he could comprehend. For Moses saw the Land, from Mount Nebo across the Dead Sea all the way up to the Lebanon and Mount Hermon – far beyond what the human eye could see. But there was more, for Moses appeared in the Promised Land, with Elijah, during the Transfiguration (Deu. 34:1-4; Mat. 17:3).

Again, we see the principle: *"For he is not a God of the dead, but of the living"* (Luke 20:37-38). This is also seen in the often quoted *"by whose stripes you were healed,"* with verse 25 speaking about souls being saved (1 Peter 2:24).

Having faith and getting saved was the primary aim and message of several healings recorded in the Gospels, for example, with the blind man of Jericho: *"Your faith has saved you"* (Luke 18:42).

For healing is temporary; Lazarus later returned to the grave. People focus on physical well-being, but foremost is the advancement of the Kingdom. It is far more about spiritual restoration than about empty hospital wards. It requires greater Kingdom-like vision, to understand that it is not so much about physical, temporal health.

Like Moses, we need to take our eyes away from the temporal to see the Promised Land – our ultimate objective is a kind of transfiguration into the holy Presence of God (Deu. 32:52; Mat. 17:3-4).

As a general rule, divine healings thus have to do with the promotion of the Kingdom and the Gospel; to confirm the authority of His servants in the eyes among the lost sheep of Israel. And *"other sheep that are not of this fold* [the Jews]," Yeshua spoke about, but is not really understood (John 10:16; Isaiah 49:6). As Peter explained: *"For you were as sheep going astray; but are now returned to the Shepherd and Overseer of your souls"* (1 Peter 2:25).

Therefore, Paul sometimes prayed for healing, as with the heathen chief on the island Melita (Malta), yet had to leave Trophimus sick on the island of Miletus and advised Timothy to drink a little wine for his ailments (Acts 28:8; 2 Tim. 4:20; 1 Tim. 5:23).

11. What does Solomon's malady teach?

A 2014-study by the Barna Group among Christians in the USA has shown that only one out of four Christians have made their faith commitment to Christ (as per the general Evangelical definition), after they have passed the age of eighteen. [ii]

Older people are much less likely to come to rebirth than young people for *"They do not cry for help when He binds them. They die [in their souls] in youth, and their life ends among the perverted persons"* (Job 36:13-14).

Years ago Radio Pulpit (South Africa) reported on a similar study, where the number of people who accepted Jesus as personal Savior dropped dramatically once the age of fifty was reached. Among the elderly of over seventy, only one was reported in the test sample. (This differs during Awakenings, when young and old reportedly queue to confess.)

People become set in their ways. The arteries and the heart harden and rebirth becomes improbable. For the chances of mind transforming-repentance and a dramatic lifestyle-change get remote once one is over forty. You must bend a tree while it is still young (Deu. 6:7, 11:19):

"Train up a child in the way he should go, and when he is old he will not depart from it" (Prov. 22:6*); "Remember also your Creator in the days of your youth, before the evil days come, and the years draw near, when you will say, 'I have no pleasure in them.'"* (Eccl. 12:1);

"I tell you, whoever will not receive the kingdom of God as a little child, he will in no way enter therein" (Mark 10:15).

The rabbis teach from Leviticus 19 that one should stand and take one's proper place before the Almighty before reaching old age: *"You shall rise before the gray headed and honor the presence of an old man, and fear your God"* (Lev. 19:32).

This should encourage the enthusiastic young missionaries of the 'New Monastic Movement,' the 'Red Letter Christians,' (many of them were active in 12,600 prayer rooms registered with '24-7 Prayer'), but there is a serious lack of Bible literacy that results in young believers falling into the trap of humanistic, self-centered spirituality.

This is especially true where there is a general familiarity with the Gospel and a lukewarm doctrine of general salvation is preached.

There is also the danger of falling away from Christ where continual growth – *"building yourselves up in your most holy faith"* – is neglected (Jude 1:20).

I call this lukewarm disease 'King Solomon's malady': It is the capacity to lose contact with Christ when disappointment, ailments, loneliness and poverty easily bring about bitterness and murmuring. Prosperity and the cares of life can turn a lukewarm Christian into ice-cold. Either we continually stoke the fires of faith, or it dies.

"For it happened, when Solomon was old, that his wives turned away his heart after other gods; and his heart was not perfect with Yahweh his God, as was the heart of David his father" (1 Kings 11:24 –WEB);

"Remember your Creator in the days of your youth, before the difficult days come, and the years draw near when you say, 'I have no pleasure in them.' While the sun and the light... are not darkened...

"Remember your Creator before the silver cord is loosed. Then the dust will return to the earth as it was, and the spirit [breath] will return to God who gave it" (Ecc. 12:1-7).

We thus seriously need to heed the warnings of NOT losing our 'First Love' – not only as individuals but also as assemblies – resulting in empty cathedrals, relics of a faith where the Spirit has departed: *"And because iniquity shall multiply, the love of many shall grow cold"* (Mat. 24:12); *"You have perseverance and have endured for my name's sake, and have not grown weary. But I have this against you, that you left your first love"* (Rev. 2:3-4);

"I know your works, that you are neither cold nor hot. I wish you were cold or hot. So, because you are lukewarm, and neither hot nor cold, I will vomit you out of my mouth" (Rev. 3:15-16).

We will all enter "life's final battle" when "death gives way to victory" to quote the words of the song 'Because He lives'. Long before that day, before old age takes its toll, we need to be sure of having secured our name in the Book of Life (Ps. 69:28-36; Rev. 3:5). [iii]

Solace is found exclusively in Yeshua our Redeemer: *"Therefore I take pleasure in infirmities, in reproaches, in necessities, in persecutions, in distresses for Christ's sake: for when I am weak, then am I strong"* (2 Cor. 12:10).

Our greatest joy, our greatest hope, is that death has been defeated (1 Cor. 15:20).

Selah.

"Because He lives, we can face tomorrow"

The famous Gospel song 'Because He lives,' written by Bill and Gloria Gaither in 1969, explains the true Christian view of victory in Christ even in suffering and in death: "And then one day, I'll cross the river, I'll fight life's final war with pain; And then, as death gives way to victory, I'll see the lights of glory and I'll know He lives!" The best rendition of this song, in my opinion, was by David Crowder and his band at the Georgia Dome in Atlanta with the Passion 2013 conference, attended by 60,000 young Christians. https://www.youtube.com/watch?v=ujUPAPQ5SZA.

Part Two: When does prayer miss the mark?

INDEX

Prayer, in itself, is a sign of faith, a sacrament of recognition: Recognizing our Father in heaven's total supremacy, even when He replies by not answering!

1. The placebo of the faithless Church?

IT is amazing how many Churches have adopted faithless doctrines regarding the most basic teachings of the New Testament, such as the command: *"Heal the sick, raise the dead, cleanse lepers, drive out demons"* (Mat. 10:7-9; Luke 10:8-9).

Many don't even have organized prayer meetings, or if they do, are formal and lack in power (Mat. 6:30, 8:26, 14:31, 16:8). Some have nurtured the concept of divine election as a 'covenant people' beyond what even the Pharisees claimed (Mat. 3:9), and took Replacement theology to an extreme, having chained the *"gifts of the Spirit"* with

Medieval theology. Bad doctrine is like whitewash on a badly plastered wall of unbelief (1 Cor. 12:1-11; Eze. 13:1-18).

The theologians of such churches defend a position of unfaith, and see 'faith healing' as either a 'placebo effect,' or as pure fraud, which it unfortunately sometimes is. Beware of those apostle-prophet-pastors who advertise 'healing on demand' (Acts 8:18-20)!

Science has come to the aid of the faithless and prayerless. One of the favorite arguments against faith or divine healing is the 'placebo effect' where tests have shown that fake medicine also elicits a response similar to the proper treatment.

Psychiatrists provide other explanations, such as conditioning, motivation, expectation, the power of suggestion and mass hypnosis. Which are all true in part among the many charlatans operating in the Church (Micah 3:11; Mat. 21:13; 2 Peter 1:1-15).

If most Christians fail to firmly believe in the Bible, why expect the world to be convinced to believe in something like the power of prayer? Which is why divine healing as the result of powerful faith and prayer is a demonstration of Kingdom power.

Where and when will they firsthand experience real healings? Not of a sore back or a headache; we are talking of cases where doctors say: "This can't be your blood test, they must have mixed it up," or "These can't be your x-rays." We're talking about the deaf hearing, the blind seeing, the dead raised.

Yet we know that the world will still doubt faith healing, just as the religious and educated people questioned the miracles of Yeshua, for example, with the blind beggar at the Temple (Mat. 9:1-41).

Why do we have this sad situation among so many Christians in so many churches? It's simply because so many are like the learned and righteous

Nicodemus, who recognized Jesus to be *"from God,"* but are not fully re-birthed by Spirit (John 3:1-21).

2. Charge the windmills like Don Quixote?

THE way the Bible gets quoted at random and "the devil's tail gets whipped" by many a good Christian reminds me of Don Quixote charging the windmills in the chivalric knight's imaginary crusade.

One must caution against this, for the Word is *"the sword of the Spirit"* (Eph. 6:17) and the Bible – like any other weapon, if used carelessly – can and will hurt: *"For the Word of God is quick, and powerful, and sharper than any two-edged sword, piercing even to the divide soul and spirit"* (Heb. 4:12).

In fact, Jeremiah wrote the Word is also like fire and a hammer, referring to the way master masons for centuries used to break rock in quarries (Jer. 23:29).

Prayer warriors must be adept at handling the Word like a two-edged sword, as part of the armor of God [YeHoVaH], which foremost means to *"withstand in the evil day, and having done all, to stand"* (Eph. 6:13). Stand firmly and remain standing until the smoke clears is often the greater valor than charging the bastions of Satan like a religious version of Don Quixote!

It is for good reason that Paul advised Timothy that elders and deacons in the assembly should not be novices in the faith (1 Tim. 3), though many unfortunately stay 'babes' till they eventually lose their teeth in old age (Eccl. 12:3).

To be "whipping the devil's tail" is a sure sign of NOT being Jude 1:8-compliant, I think. To be Jude 1:8-compliant is to have a sense of reverence for the heavenly, not insulting that of which we have limited understanding. The biggest and very common Don Quixote-mistake is to do 'verse hunting,' to search the Bible only for those verses that 'suits the mood' and fit the doctrine.

Don Quixote

The famous novel 'The Ingenious Gentleman Don Quixote of La Mancha' by Miguel de Cervantes. Part one was first published in 1605 in Spain.

3. A message with Bible roulette?

AN equally dangerous method is to combine a number of random verses as a 'message from God.' And yet, to my amazement, this is how I have seen some evangelicals operate. Such a technique is suspect and should be treated as a highly irregular exception at best.

So, let me qualify the statement: The haphazard selection of Bible verses for divine guidance could be as hazardous as Russian roulette. Be very cautious, for the heart is unreliable, as Jeremiah says: *"The heart is deceitful above all things, and desperately sick; who can understand it?"* (Jer. 17:9).

Think of how Eve, who was perfect and knew no sin, yet wanting to know more, got deceived (Gen. 3:5). Beware that the heart does not mislead to confirm what one would like to hear (Ps. 64:6c).

Yes, we all get pulled out of the lake a couple of times when we, like Peter, try to walk on water in faith, but we must be very careful on how we use the Word-sword. And beware of persons who too easily claim, 'the Lord says' and 'the Lord told me so.'

'Bible roulette' is when believers in a prayer group or a 'home-cell' take turns to quote Bible verses that 'have spoken to them' that day and then combine the various verses to formulate what they believe to be a message from God.

Yes, every believer should be able to say what verse from the Bible spoke into their soul that day, there is no problem with that, the danger is to go around and around and then haphazardly combine numerous Bible verses, concluding with an assumed divine message.

I still hear the pastor enthusiastically claim: *"Mmm, awesome! I feel the Lord says..."* And then he made up some story. This was of course done with piety, but do we see such an example in Scripture?

4. Liberal grace and universal prayer?

PRAYER connects humankind to a spiritual dimension that is far beyond simple comprehension, but the conversation or communication must be on the terms of the Almighty, not so?

Humankind is free to worship what they want and how they want, but have you seriously evaluated the mountain of historic evidence regarding the God of Israel compared to other famed or alleged deities? When you do so, consider the reason for the vile criticism and open attacks from every quarter on our religion.

Our prayers should thus be to 'awaken' those who are asleep, before it is too late, before the flesh succumbs to its mortality: *"Therefore he says, "Awake, you who sleep, and arise from the dead, and Christ will shine on you"* (Eph. 5:14).

Our prayers should be for repentance and life to the lost, for the gift of faith is only possible through Yeshua the Redeemer (Eph. 2:8-9). He is *"the Face"* of the Almighty who is invisible (Col. 1:15; John 1:18), the Restorer of man's lost connection to our heavenly Father (Mark 14:36; Gal. 4:6).

If we take the often-quoted 2 Chronicles 7:14 and put aside Romans 11 and Replacement theology, the first steps of putting faith into practice are humble repentance and prayer: *"If My people, which are called by My name, will humble themselves, pray, seek My face, and turn from their wicked ways; then I will hear from heaven, will forgive their sin, and will heal their land."*

To assume that universal prayer and 'ecumenical unity' would impress the Almighty would be wrong, for it is not the quantity of prayer, the eloquence, or the number of people praying that counts.

One attribute of the God of Israel is that He is 'jealous,' a 'consuming fire' (Ex. 34:14). The history of Israel shows that any form of worship of the gods of other nations was an abomination. Why pray to something created by man and or demon? There is absolutely no reason or excuse for promoting 'ecumenical unity' and global prayer with other religions (1 Cor.10:20; 1 Tim. 4:1).

The only way to know God the Father, who is Spirit (John 4:24), is through Christ Jesus, *"the Word that became flesh and dwelt among us"* (John 1:14). If we know Yeshua as Messiah, then we know the Father (John 6:44-14:9-14; Col. 2:9).

We should never misinterpret grace as an excuse for continued sin. Beware of the twisted grace of pop-theology that claims God's love through Jesus, but lacks in reverence for God's Word, failing to understand that He, as the Word of God, is both grace and faith (Acts 3:16; Heb. 12:2). True confessional repentance always results in good fruit, in a changed life away from old sins.

Beware of scoffers who call the faith-response of getting born-again and baptized as "jumping through theological hoops."

Was Abraham's circumcision 'works,' or the result of his faith? (Rom. 4:1-10). Yes, it is by grace that we receive God's gift of life (Eph. 2:8-9); but finding the 'Narrow Way' and staying on it requires similar faith-decisions.

The danger of falling away, of professing grace without the fruit of a Redeemed-life, is what many warnings in the New Testament are all about. True repentance changes lives, as in the example of Matthew the tax collector, who immediately displayed the fruit of repentance (Mat. 9:9-13; Mark 2:14-17; Luke 5:27-32).

Following Christ is what turns people away from their wicked ways and eventually causes nations to change their morals and destiny. However, when and where the Gospel is compromised, the Church loses its influence as salt loses its flavor (Mat. 5:13).

Beware of the wolf packs of theology that tear at the Bible, preaching a humanistic Gospel: *"He that turns away his ear from hearing the law, even his prayer shall be abomination"* (Prov. 28:9); but: *"Knowing this, that the law is not made for a righteous man, but for the lawless and disobedient"* (1 Tim. 1:9).

Beware of those who talk about Jesus but are disrespectful of the entire Bible as the Almighty's revealed opinion and His preference about man's habits and manners.

First in the Scriptures of the Old Testament with its covenants and then in the New Testament, revealing *"the Law of the Spirit of life in Christ Jesus"* that defeats the *"law of sin and death"* (Rom. 8:2), but does not abolish God's revealed opinion on what defines righteousness, holy living and what is pleasing in His sight.

"Woe to the world because of offenses! For offenses must come, but woe to that man by whom the offense comes!" (Mat. 18:7). The most foul enemies are those perceived to be saintly, but are anti-God's Law – the trademark of the lost, of those promoting the antichrist's agenda is their persistent attacks on Biblical values (1 John 1:7, 2:18-22, 4:3).

Without law, no fair judgement can be passed on evil. And without divine judgement there is no righteousness, and without righteousness there can be no goodness and this we know cannot be, for God – and only God – is good (Luke 18:19)!

Are our prayers not heard because we interpret and break God's rules just as we please? Have we been freed from sin to continue with a worldly lifestyle and fashion? Are we conformed to Christ's nature, or our old nature? (Rom. 12:1-2). Are we transformed in Christ or fixated on questionable doctrines and old wine-skin-traditions?

We, who sincerely believe in the Risen Messiah, who are truly born-again, obey the commandments of Yeshua by spirit – His Word becomes our DNA – and the prayer of such brethren have been proved to be worthy of being presented by angels to the throne of the Almighty (Rev. 8:3-4).

5. Asking or a 'creed of greed'?

IN John 14:14 Jesus said, *"Whatever you may ask in My name, that I will do... If you ask anything in My name, I will do it."* And in John 15:16: *"Whatever you shall ask of the Father in My name, He may give it to you."* And: *"If you have faith like a mustard seed... nothing will be impossible for you"* (Mat. 17:15-21).

All we see or hear in the above verses are 'whatever we ask' and 'nothing shall be impossible for you' – not so?! It just shows how deceptive the heart is (Jer. 17:9).

Yes, anything is possible where faith and the prayer of a righteous believer combine. But if John 14 and 15 are quoted fully and in context, we see these Scriptures are about prayer for *"the Father to be glorified in the Son"* and to *"bring forth fruit."*

It is speaking about receiving grace to walk on 'the Way' (Acts 24:14), not to satisfy the 'lust of thy eye,' not so?

"For all that is in the world, the lust of the flesh, and the lust of the eyes, and the pride of life, is not of the Father, but is of the world" (1 John 2:16); *"This I say then, walk in the Spirit, and you shall not fulfill the lust of the flesh"* (Gal. 5:16).

How often is the focus of prayer and worship on man and not on God? How often is it about 'me' and 'I'? Sure, we can say, *"I can do all things through Christ"* (Phil. 4:13); or *"we are more than conquerors"* (Romans 8:37) – which is true because these words are in the Bible – but dare we make a mantra of Bible verses quoted half and out of context?

Ask, for example, any Evangelical about 'Jabez' and they can quote 1 Chronicles 4: *"Jabez called on the God of Israel, saying, "Oh that you would bless me indeed, and enlarge my border! May your hand be with me, and may you keep me from evil, that I may not cause pain!" God granted him that which he requested"* (1 Chr. 4:10).

A booklet by Bruce Wilkinson in 2001, probably inspired by a classic sermon by Charles Spurgeon (1834-1892), sold by the million and the 'Jabez Prayer' quickly became a credo for America's 'Word of Faith' millionaires-in-the-make, copied by other prosperity preachers across the globe.

If only they would have listened to Spurgeon's sermon, for he said: "The dreariest deserts in Christendom are those places that were fertilized by the obvious manures of certain revivalists."

Another example of faith and of asking is Caleb's daughter Othniel: *"Caleb said, "What do you want?" She said, "Give me a blessing. Because you have set me in the land of the South, give me also springs of water." So he gave her the upper springs and the lower springs"* (Josh. 15:14-19).

We thus need to discern the seasons; when to be content and when to be like Jabez and Othniel and to ask with confidence. To speak the Word of faith and ask both the fountains of the low and the highlands. But when does 'prophetic prayer' turn into the ridiculous and into incantations?

Is a 'perverse generation' only those of unbelief, or also those who see Bible verses as recipes, chanting mantra-like, or the Balaam of Peor-types whose skewed knowledge of God becomes perverse in application? (Num. 22:8-32).

Is this not where the 'seed principle' of faith has developed into a 'creed for greed' among those preachers who have made selecting verses out of context an art – much the same way the enemy quoted Scripture with the Temptation of Messiah? (Luke 4:1-13).

Prosperity preachers are quick to mention that Abraham, Jacob, Joseph and Solomon prospered; true, the word 'rich' appears 80 times in the Bible, but 90% of the time in a negative sense! This, too, is to test our hearts.

They never quote James 2:5: *"Listen, my beloved brothers, has not God chosen those who are poor in the world to be rich in faith and heirs of the kingdom, which he has promised to those who love him?"*

We all share in the redemption in Christ, but those saints who spend their lives in luxurious grace, while preaching fervently on tithing, except the Pilgrim's Tithe and giving that every third year to the local widows and orphans (Deu. 14:22-29; 26:).

Isn't it amazing that Moses used the word 'tithe' only seven times, yet, pastors who are fast to denounce the Old Testament as historic and obsolete preach grace and tithing seven times a month!

Does it not reveal a deep, basic dishonesty? Does it not remind one of handsome Absalom's plans to take the kingdom? (2 Sam. 15:1-14). *"Be free from the love of money, content with such things as you have"* (Heb. 13:5).

"Not that I speak because of lack, for I have learned in whatever state I am, to be content in it" (Phil. 4:11); *"But having food and clothing, we will be content with that"* (1 Tim. 6:8); *"You ask, and receive not, because you ask amiss, that you may consume it upon your lusts"* (James 4:3).

<u>The 'creed of greed' using the 'seed principle'</u>

There is a fine line between faith and the 'seed principle' being applied as a 'creed of greed,' where the focus of many is on themselves and not the Kingdom, as taught in the parable of the mustard seed (Mat. 17:20). Our faith is like seed, when we release it the Almighty changes our (souls') nature and ultimately one day we too will be resurrected as 'a new creature'. First, a measure of faith is needed (Rom. 12:3); second, faith comes alive by *"hearing... hearing the Word of YeHoVaH"* (Rom. 10:17); thirdly, a deed of faith – a word to the mountain – is required. 'Faith without works is dead'. James 2:17-18: *"Even so faith, if it has not works, is dead, being alone."* The 'creed of greed' – where the Word is not truly applied for Kingdom purposes – is much the same as religious works without Kingdom-purpose at heart. King David introduced many rituals and 'beautified the feasts,' which would have been rated as 'works,' if it was not that his sole purpose was to glorify the 'Kingdom of Heaven' and had confirmation via the seer and prophet of his day (1 Chron. 15:16; 2 Chron. 35:15; Neh.12:45-46; Wisdom of Sirach 47:10).

God [YeHoVaH] gave Adam dominion on earth and told Adam to *"dress and keep"* the Garden (Gen. 2:15, 19). One cannot be a gardener and not understand the 'seed principle,' for it is the core of our daily provision, but one cannot love one divine principle and ignore the next, can one? What about *"thou shall not covet"*? (Ex. 20:17).

But yes, prayer warriors should understand the principle of seed and faith, for our prayers are like seed sown in faith. Sometimes we see a large harvest in a short time, but other seed needs to be treated first and stay dormant for a very long time before the miracle of life occurs. The key of faith is to unlock the treasures of the Kingdom of Heaven and not to chase after the things of the world.

The world, however, hates to see a prosperous pastor; they hate to see a man of God that is not beggarly poor. There are about 3,000 billionaires on the planet and millions of evil men who have enriched themselves at great cost to humanity and earth, but a single super-dynamic Christian pastor owns an airplane and he gets investigated.

True believers are, as people who are 'dead' to this world, not easily enticed by 'bling' and things that have no Kingdom value.

There is nothing wrong with having a nice house or farm, because God blesses hard, honest work, but ultimately, our first priority is to make sure one has a room reserved in the Kingdom.

We need to realize that everything is grace — the health and wisdom and the opportunities that came our way were due to grace and probably the faith and prayers of previous generations, *"showing loving kindness to thousands of those who love me and keep my commandments"* (Exo. 20:6; Deu. 7:6).

We are to honor our Father in heaven, for all we have, always remembering the parable of the rich young ruler (Mark 14:36; Mat. 19). The final word came from Yeshua in Luke 12:15: *"Take heed and beware of covetousness, for one's life does not consist in the abundance of the things he possesses."*

Let me conclude with this warning from Spurgeon:"Beware," Spurgeon said, "Beware of presuming that you are saved. If you merely say, "I believe in Jesus," it does not save you. If your heart is truly renewed, if you hate the things that you once loved, and love the things that you once hated; if you have really repented; if there is a complete change of mind in you; if you are born again, then you have reason to rejoice.

But if there is no real change, no inward godliness; if there is no love to God, no prayer, no work of the Holy Spirit, then your saying, "I am saved," is nothing but your own assertion, and it may delude, but it will not deliver you.

"Our prayer ought to be, "Oh, that you would bless me, with real faith, with real salvation, with the trust in Jesus — that is the essential of faith; not with the conceit that produces a lack of caution. God preserves us from imaginary blessings!" Spurgeon warned of believers who never end their prayers with "Not my will, but your will."

6. Should silence discourage?

OF course, children can ask, but a Father can also refuse or choose to ignore, not so? The "ask and thou shall be given" promises of Jesus had to do with the future work in spreading the Gospel. The works, the signs, the miracles have always been for the verification of authenticity in the promotion of the Kingdom of God (Acts 4:30).

There are many, many more miracles being done today in the name of Jesus/ Yeshua than ever before in history, because it is the same Holy Spirit that is in operation and the harvest belongs to our Father and our King (John 14:12-14).

John 21:25 says that there were many miracles by Yeshua not recorded. So, how many were recorded?

The four Gospels recorded thirty-five miracles, of which twenty-one involved healings, two multiplications and three raised from the dead by Yeshua. Note that each of these recorded events taught a specific Kingdom principle.

The number of recorded miracles

If the duration of the ministry of Jesus was about 30 to 36 months, as is generally assumed, the number of recorded miracles would average only one per month and two Passovers were then not reported on. The alternative is to consider that John 6:4 was either a scribal error or an insertion. It could have referred to another of the six Jewish feasts (Lev. 23), or an insertion by Eusebius of Caesarea (260 to 339 AD). The rabbis consider 'Tabernacles' at the end of the 49-day Omer count as the proper end of the Passover season, which links the two feasts. In such a case, John's Gospel is a precise recording of every feast in Jerusalem, including Hanukkah. Before Eusebius, the early Church held the short view. It would also explain why the other three Gospels also recorded only the last Passover. It points to a ministry date of between 27 and 30 AD – Hosea 6:2's 'two days' for the Gentiles prophecy is close to expiry. Read that with Luke 21:24.

Luke 11:5-13 actually explains the issue best; after teaching the 'Lord's prayer,' the following well-known parables about prayer were given:

The persistent lender-neighbor who demanded bread at midnight, the earthly father who will not give his child a stone for bread, or a snake for fish, or a scorpion for an egg. But with what does Yeshua conclude?

"If you then, being evil, know how to give good gifts to your children, how much more will your heavenly Father give the Holy Spirit to those who ask Him" (Luke 11:13)!

The primary aim of the teaching was thus not to ask for material things, *"for your heavenly Father knows that you have need of all these things,"* but to ask for the Holy Spirit to empower spiritual growth and pursue the Kingdom in our prayers (Mat. 6:32)!

Plenty of examples of times when the prayers of ancient Israel were not heard, serve as warnings for us (1 Cor. 10:11).

Take, for instance, Luke 4: *"There were many widows in Israel in Elijah's time. It had not rained for three-and-a-half years, and the famine was severe everywhere in the country. But the Lord didn't send Elijah to anyone except a widow at Zarephath in the territory of Sidon.*

"There were also many people with skin diseases in Israel in the prophet Elisha's time. But the Lord cured no one except Naaman from Syria" (Luke 4:25-27).

Now think about it – how many prayers and sacrifices were made to the Almighty for rain during a drought of three years? How many widows in Israel would have been weeping desperately? How many lepers, suffering the dreaded disease with its impurity and societal rejection, would have been equally distraught?

So, why pray if God knows your situation, but nothing happens? Because prayer is in itself a faith-sign, a sacrament of recognition: Recognizing our Father in heaven's total supremacy, even when He answers by not answering!

There are at least two reasons for what may appear like silence: Covenant-breaking sin and the sparrow-promise (Mat. 10:29-31).

One, for the majority, He says: My children, review your life, review broken covenants, review pet doctrines, review your pleas and then return to Me.

Take the case of a three-year drought in the days of King David, when prayer revealed that it was because King Saul had broken the covenant with the Gibeonites (2 Sam. 21:1-14). If a covenant with a deceitful tribe was so important, what about our covenantal promises to God: Those made in the Church at weddings, conversion and baptism?

Unless this is done, there could – proven by Biblical history – come a day when the reply is not what the unrepentant would like to hear: *"When you spread out your hands, I will hide my eyes from you. Yes, when you make many prayers, I will not hear. Your hands are full of blood [sin]. Wash yourselves, make yourself clean..."* (Isa. 1:15-16); *"Do not plead with me, for I will not listen to you"* (Jer. 7:16b).

The answer to the individual or the clan is thus this: Review your life, your case and your prayer – correct that which is wrong and then submit your plea again.

Two, the sparrow-promise: For the righteous, those who love God and live according to His Word, there is the assurance that their tears and laments have been noticed and recorded on the scroll (Ps. 56:8).

In fact, and in faith, we believe that God's response has been set in motion, even when – as the prophet Habakkuk concluded – the sheep stalls are still empty (Hab. 3:17-19).

Like Hannah, after travailing in prayer – even in a whisper – we can return home with a changed countenance, knowing that the God of Israel hears the prayers of the barren (1 Sam. 1:20). As in Daniel 9:23, we believe that our prayers are heard the moment we go on our knees. It is just the visible result that sometimes takes time.

Times of barrenness, when our prayers seem to be unanswered – as in the prayers for a child for Sarah, Rebecca and Hannah – draw us closer to God, to unite us in travailing, persistent prayer to Him.

Do therefore not be discouraged when years and years of prayer for loved ones to come to faith, for children to love Yeshua and get married to Godly spouses, seem to go unanswered. The long wait is sometimes because the best ceramic pots are those that stay in the potter's fire the longest!

The reason for persisting is that the prayers of the weak, the humble, of orphans and widows, but yes, even the prayers of sinners, do touch His heart. We can indeed, like the distraught father of a boy suffering from epilepsy-like symptoms, cry with all honesty: *"I believe; help thou my unbelief [weak faith]"* (Mark 9:24).

Take the classic example of Israel, suffering as slaves in Egypt: *"I have surely seen the affliction of my people which are in Egypt, and have heard their cry by reason of their taskmasters; for I know their sorrows"* (Ex. 3:7).

"The righteous cry out, and the LORD [YeHoVaH] hears, and delivers them out of all their troubles. The LORD [YeHoVaH] is near to those who have a broken heart, and saves such as have a contrite [crushed, humble] spirit. Many are the afflictions of the righteous, but the LORD [YeHoVaH] delivers him out of them all" (Ps. 34:17-19).

7. Did martyrs lack prosper-faith?

'PRIDE of life,' 'idols of the heart' and self-indulgence are general ills among many where the easy-grace 'Gospel of accommodation' prospers, often with much music and little substance.

Many a popular doctrine is based on partial truth (quoting from the Bible, which is truth, but ignoring other Bible verses and context), keeping a flock of 'babes' that are easy to control, to indoctrinate and 'fleece,' as the bad shepherds do. The true shepherd grows his flock, knowing that factual (worldly) truth does not equal spiritual (Biblical) truth.

The remedy is to proclaim Yeshua's Gospel, making Him the center of preaching and prayer; not the family, not marriage, not the youth, not music, not parenting, not welfare, not the SPCA or any other 'ministry'.

Prayer and preaching must be Kingdom focused (Luke 11:1-13), for the rest are temporary stuff: *"You ask, and don't receive, because you ask amiss, so that you may spend it for your pleasures"* (James 4:3).

Paul's testimony – and that of the original martyr Church – is and was very remote from the indulgence and promotion of affluence in the Western Church.

As Brother Yun of China, author of 'The Heavenly Man' (pages 296-297), has noticed: "It seems you want to stop and enjoy His presence and blessings too long, and build an altar to your experiences."

Where the focus is on Yeshua and the Kingdom, blessing is not measured by the values of the world and prayer is aimed at prosperity in Spirit and not the stuff that makes decadence prosper, knowing that to become the 'full measure of Christ' is to outgrow the need for bling and a superficial credit- and flesh-bound life.

"For the wicked boasts of his heart's cravings, he blesses the greedy," *"Surely the mind and heart of man are cunning"* (Ps. 10:3, 64:6c).

Consider the testimony of the martyr believers of the early Church:

"But in all things we commend ourselves as ministers of God: In much patience, in tribulations, in needs, in distresses, in stripes, in imprisonments, in tumults, in labors, in sleeplessness, in fastings; by purity, by knowledge, by long-suffering, by kindness, by the Holy Spirit, by sincere love, by the word of truth, by the power of God...

"As unknown, and yet well known; as dying, and behold we live; as chastened, and yet not killed; as sorrowful, yet always rejoicing; as poor, yet

making many rich; as having nothing, and yet possessing all things" (2 Cor. 6:4-10).

Was Paul's faith too small? Was the faith of martyrs too little? Or is the prosper-message of many pastors not unwittingly aimed at the 'pride of life'? Are they being deceived by the idols of their hearts?

Prosperity teaching is so in conflict with the servant-teaching of Jesus in Luke 17:6-10, for example, whose merit and works as plowman or shepherd is in Messiah alone. Prosperity is a doctrine that fails at the gates of adversity and it will probably not be long before these prophet-preachers among the affluent will be proved false.

Believers should rather trust Paul's message and be ready, yet never fearful and never promote conspiracies, but know *"That we must through much tribulation enter into the kingdom of God"* (Act 14:22); *"For verily, when we were with you, we told you before that we should suffer tribulation; even as it came to pass, and you know"* (1 The. 3:4).

When claims are made about the 'Bride' to be ready for an imminent departure to heaven, the reality of her blemished dress and ignorance is on display. Equally so are dozens of outstanding Bible prophecies regarding Jacob's gathering overlooked and misapplied.

Prayer warriors must be vigilant, for we experience much grace and many blessings, but the 'crown of life' is only received at the 'prize-giving' in *"the kingdom prepared"* at the end (Mat. 25:34). What fraud would it be to hand out medals at the start of a marathon, not so?

If backsliding from the faith was impossible (as some allege), thinking the 'narrow Way' is like a railway track to heaven (Mat. 7:14), why then the repeated warnings to the seven Assemblies of the Apocalypse? (Rev. 1-3).

"Remember therefore from where you have fallen, and repent and do the first works…"; "As many as I love, I reprove and chasten. Be zealous therefore, and repent." (Rev. 2:5, 3:19); "Blessed is the man who endures temptation; for when he has been approved, he will receive the crown of life which the Lord has promised to those who love Him" (James 1:12).

Those who deny Yeshua as God – the typical ex-Christian converts to either Judaism or the New Age self-spirituality or worse, the worldly scoffers and the neo-pagans with their 'un-baptism' ceremonies, they all surely grieve the Spirit, not so?

"Therefore, I tell you, every sin and blasphemy will be forgiven men, but the blasphemy against the Spirit will not be forgiven men.

"Whoever speaks a word against the Son of Man, it will be forgiven him; but whoever speaks against the Holy Spirit, it will not be forgiven him, neither in this age, nor in that which is to come" (Mat. 12:30-32).

<u>How to recognize the false Christ</u>

The final false messiah will do healings and wonders, but not in the name of Yeshua and cannot fulfill prophecies relating to the true Messiah (Mat. 24:24). The world will welcome this false saviour, but the saints will not be fooled: *"Be not to be quickly shaken in your mind, and not be troubled, either by spirit, or by word… even he whose coming is according to the working of Satan with all power and signs and lying wonders"* (2 Thes. 2:2, 9).

That said, those who threaten others about 'grieving the Holy Spirit,' should read Ephesians 4, for there is often a false sense of self-righteousness and religious pride:

"Let no corrupt word proceed out of your mouth, but what is good for necessary edification, that it may impart grace to the hearers. And grieve not the Holy Spirit of God, whereby you are sealed to the day of redemption.

"Let all bitterness, wrath, anger, clamor, and evil speaking be put away from you, with all malice. And be you kind one to another, tenderhearted, forgiving one another, even as God for Christ's sake has forgiven you" (Eph. 4:29-31).

Selah.

How then shall we Pray? 80 core essence issue – Series

Book 1: Prayer as the power of faith

1. The basics of prayer

- What is prayer really?
- Is it a duty or privilege to pray?
- What examples are there?
- What attitude is required for prayer?
- What prayer stirs Awakenings?
- What is the Hebrew view?
- What do we learn from Jacob?
- Are our prayers 'musty spices'?
- How to grow in the 'fullness of Christ'?
- What does the 'Lord's Prayer' teach?
- What causes prayer failure?
- How much to pray about an issue?

2. Clear the muddy water

- Is there religious zeal or new life?
- Why the need to hear the rooster's crow?
- Whose name is written in the sand?
- What do we learn from Moses?
- Why 'faith baptism' with grace?
- So, how does the Spirit gain dominion?

- What is man and soul without rebirth?
- Why doubt the testimony of saints?
- Why the modest 'Prayer of Salvation'?
- Why fear to find the Comforter?

3. Get on the chariot

- Why get on Elijah's chariot?
- How do 'prayer warriors' get drafted?
- Nehemiah: What can others teach us?
- What did the 'miracle mermaid' pray?
- Why the need for 'boiler room' prayer?
- Why should 'two or more' pray?
- Why intercede for Sodom?
- How do the Karoo farmers pray?

Book 2: The Word as sword of truth

1. In whose name do we pray?

- To whom should we direct prayer?
- In whose Name should we ask?
- Did the Jews call Him 'Yeshua'?
- Why call Me 'Baal,' Lord or Allah?
- When shall 'My people know My Name?'

2. Taking up the sword

- How to take up the 'sword of the Spirit'?
- Can fasting be neglected?
- Why not follow Daniel's example?

- How to have 'a clean heart'?
- How do we get the Bride spotless?
- Why not kneel if possible?
- Why make a covenant with one's eyes?
- Why do some use a prayer shawl?

3. The laying on of hands and 'tongues'

- Is there pride in the humble confession?
- Up to what point should we pray?
- Why the laying on of hands?
- Why pray in a heavenly language?
- Why is boldness the forgotten ingredient?

Book 3: Faith healing explained

1. How do we pray for healing?

- Why is faith-healing always Plan A?
- Why are the hospitals not empty?
- Why blunt the sword's blade?

- Why more miracles on the mission field?
- How do we judge the use of gifts?
- What if a dark place is part of the plan?
- What can we learn from Wigglesworth?
- Have we really done all we can?
- When is prayer preparation for victory?
- Do we share in paranoia about death?
- What was Solomon's malady?

2. When do prayers miss the mark?

- The placebo of the faithless Church.
- Why charge the windmills like Don Quixote?
- Why avoid liberal grace, universal prayer?
- When is asking a 'creed for greed'?
- Why should silence not discourage?
- Did the martyrs lack prosper-faith?

Book 4: Why worship went wrong

1. What song is in the Vineyard?

- Why has the band replaced the pulpit?
- Should the Church or culture change?
- What song is heard in the Vineyard?
- What can we learn from David's band?
- So, is it fashion or breakthrough?
- What is missing in the music mix?

2. So, does truth really matter?

- Lost in a labyrinth concealing truth?
- What about the girdle of truth?
- Why can't the 'little foxes' count nothing?
- Why call David's grandma a harlot?
- What is the Nicolaitan evil?
- Do we love enough not to be eccentric?

3. How do we correct and teach?

- Should we know the depths of darkness?
- Why avoid brethren-bashing?
- How to keep good company?
- Where should the loyalty of the saints be?
- Why is Israel the dividing line?

Book 5: Visions in the mirror of prophecy

1. Why ignore the dim mirror?

- Why did Messiah not prevent Judas?
- How fair is divine election?
- When is the 'fullness of the Gentiles'?
- When shall Ezekiel's cane mend?
- So, where is this remnant?
- Why presume perfect vision?

2. How to apply binding & loosing

- Are the 'ghost busters' real?
- Can you bind a servant spirit?
- What about 'binding and loosing'?
- What is 'Kingly intercession'?

3. The prophetic dimension

- When is the prophetic gift abused?
- What examples do we have?
- When does faith change nations?
- What do we pray in times of calamity?
- Why does accuracy not validate?

4. Why restore our 'Adam-hood'?

- Why the name 'Ben Adam'?
- Why the two silver trumpets?
- What's after the 'binding of Satan'?
- So, is this the 6th, 7th or 8th age?
- And who is 'Yeshurun'?

Endnotes:

[i] **Why do only some get healed?** = Dan Mohler and Tod White spoke at a 'Q&A event' in 2011 that dealt with faith healing. It can be seen at: https://www.youtube.com/watch?v=0MOJBxaKWXo. Retrieved on July, 2016.

[ii] **Demographics of conversions to Christ** = A 2014 study by the Barna Research Group indicated that nearly half of all Americans who 'accepted Jesus Christ as Saviour' did so before reaching the age of 13 (43%). From https://www.barna.org/barna-update/article/5-barna-update/196-evangelism-is-most-effective-among-kids#.VY5yZUAw98Q.

[iii] **"Because He lives"** = Composed by William and Gloria Gaither, 1971. My favorite version is this live performance by David Crowder at: https://www.youtube.com/watch?v=ujUPAPQ5SZA.

www.ingramcontent.com/pod-product-compliance
Lightning Source LLC
Chambersburg PA
CBHW050601160726
48003CB00002B/987